16
Commentaries
on the
Book of Genesis

16
Commentaries
on the
Book of Genesis

by

Frank D. Allen, PhD

authorHOUSE®

AuthorHouse™
1663 Liberty Drive
Bloomington, IN 47403
www.authorhouse.com
Phone: 1 (800) 839-8640

Published by AuthorHouse 08/05/2015

ISBN: 978-1-5049-2497-9 (sc)
ISBN: 978-1-5049-2496-2 (e)

Print information available on the last page.

*Any people depicted in stock imagery provided by Thinkstock are models,
and such images are being used for illustrative purposes only.
Certain stock imagery © Thinkstock.*

This book is printed on acid-free paper.

Contents

Introduction... vii

Summary ix

Commentary No. 1   The Death of Methuselah 1

Commentary No. 2   The Birth Order of Noah's Sons....................... 3

Commentary No. 3   The Hebrews.. 4

Commentary No. 4   Abraham, Sarah and Lot 6

Commentary No. 5   Abraham, Ishmael and Isaac............................ 9

Commentary No. 6   Lot's Fate and Legacy 12

Commentary No. 7   Isaac and Rebeka... 14

Commentary No. 8   Esau's Wives 17

Commentary No. 9   Say to Them, You are My Sister....................19

Commentary No. 10   Jacob and Laban... 21

Commentary No. 11   Jacob Meets Esau 28

Commentary No. 12   The Rape of Dinah 31

Commentary No. 13   The Death of Rachel and Birth of Benjamin.....33

Commentary No. 14   Joseph-From Slave to Governor 35

Commentary No. 15   Jacob's Sons go to Egypt to buy Grain............. 41

Commentary No. 16   Jacob's Family Moves to Egypt....................... 45

Introduction

The author of the following commentaries on the book of Genesis is not a biblical scholar and has not reviewed a single passage of the bible in it original language. Instead he has relied solely on the expertise of others in the many various English translations. In reading the bible, the author does not take the approach of a clergyman or bible teacher trying to ferret out some moral application. Instead the author approaches reading the bible consistent with his background as an engineer who has spent a long career in the development of engineering systems. In so doing, he honed the skill of reading a document in a way that continually compares what is being read currently with everything that has previously been read. The comparisons are specifically geared toward the four areas of 1) compliance, 2) compatibility, 3) completion and 4) the presence of anomalous conditions. In reading the bible as with any other document, the author has gravitated toward applying these skills, possibly sometimes subconsciously. In many parts of the bible, but especially in the book of Genesis, this approach yields such an abundance of material the author felt persuaded to summarize it for others who may be interested.

Summary

The book of Genesis divides readily into two parts. Part 1 (chapters 1-11) consists of the creation beginning with Adam and Eve in the Garden of Eden until their fall from grace. Subsequently an expanding population from Adam and Eve turned wicked in the eyes of the Lord and got slated for destruction. The Lord chose a flood as the means by which it was to be destroyed. The Lord found righteousness in a man named Noah nine generations removed from Adam and exempted him and his family from the destruction.

The Lord instructed Noah to build an Ark to withstand flood and to place in the ark a male and female of every type of living creature. The people that went aboard the ark were Noah and his wife his three sons Ham, Shem and Japeth and their wives. After the flood the progeny of Noah's sons went about the task of repopulating the earth. Nine generations removed from Noah through the line of Shem heralded the birth of Abram (Abraham) which begins part 2 of Genesis, the Patriarchal history (chapters 12-50). Only the first three commentaries deal with part 1. Commentary 1 discusses the coincidental occurrence of the death of Noah's grandfather Methuselah and the start of the flood. Commentary 2 explores the apparent confusion in translation in determining whether Shem or Japheth is the elder son of Noah. Finally, Commentary 3 tries looking at the origin of the term Hebrew and puts forth the suggestion that there is a dearth in the accounting for the number of people with that label.

Commentaries 4 through 16 all deal with part 2. Commentaries 4 through 7 cover the time period from when Abraham left his father's house to go out on his own until his grandson Jacob leaves home to seek a wife among his mother's people. More details of the events that took place in this period follow.

This period began with Abraham, his wife Sarah and his nephew Lot leaving Abraham's father's house and follows their exploits through the birth of Abraham's son Ishmael, Lot's narrow escape in the destruction of Sodom and Gomorrah and the birth of Isaac when Abraham was 100 and Sarah was 90. After the death of Sarah, Abraham, not wanting Isaac to marry a Canaanite woman sent his servant to seek a wife for him from among his people in Paddan Aram. The Servant returned with Rebekah as a wife for Isaac.

After twenty years, Rebekah gave birth to twin sons, Esau and Jacob. The two boys grew up quite differently. Esau was an outdoors type while Jacob was more of a homebody. Esau married two Canaanite women much to the displeasure of his parents. Noting the effect on them Esau sought and married the daughter of his uncle Ishmael as a third wife. Meanwhile, Jacob with the aid of his mother Rebekah tricked a nearly blind Isaac into giving the blessing intended for Esau to Jacob. This compounded by other prior bad relationships with Jacob infuriated Esau to the extent that he vowed to kill him. Then, both to avoid Jacob being killed by Esau and to assuage their disdain for Canaanite women, Isaac and Rebekah sent Jacob off to Paddan Aram to seek a wife among Rebekah's people. These events conclude at the end of Commentary 7.

Commentary 8 lays out in detail the well known confusion in the multiplicity in naming of Esau's three wives. No commentary or suggestion is offered for that confusion. It is what it is.

Commentary 9 discusses and comments on the eerie similarities in the accounts of Abraham and Isaac trying to pass off their respective wives as their sisters both for safety and political advantage. It appears that the same event may be being considered at a different time under supposedly different circumstances.

Commentaries 10 through 16 cover the events in Jacob's life until its end at age of 147. He died in Egypt after having his family brought there by his prodigious son Joseph to save the family from a famine in Canaan. The events of commentaries 10 through 16 In somewhat more detail form follow commencing in commentary 10 with Jacob on his way to Paddan Aram to seek a wife and to avoid the wrath of his brother Esau. The remaining commentaries 11 through 16 all deal with the continuing saga of Jacob and his progeny.

Upon arriving in Paddan Aram, Jacob met and was enthralled by the lovely Rachel, the daughter of his mother's brother Laban. Jacob offered to work for Laban seven years to have Rachel as his wife. At the end of the seven years, Laban tricked Jacob and gave him his older, less desirable daughter Leah as a wife but then said he could also have Rachel as well for an additional seven years of labor. Both Leah and Rachel came with their own hand maidens who became Jacob's concubines. Over the next seven years the four women provided Jacob with eleven sons and one daughter. The only daughter Dinah was Leah's seventh child and the youngest child was Joseph who was Rachel's only child born in Paddan Aram.

At the end of 14 years with Laban, Jacob made a deal with him where Jacob would accept as payment for his services the spotted and speckled animals born to the flock so they could be easily identified. With a bit of chicanery on both sides, over the next six years, Jacob built up quite a sizable flock much to the chagrin of Laban whose flock did not fare nearly as well. Realizing that Laban's attitude toward him had changed, Jacob waited until Laban was away shearing sheep and took his family and all his possession and headed back toward his father's home in Canaan. When Laban returned and found Jacob gone, he pursued him and eventually caught up to him. There was a heated confrontation which eventually ended up with them agreeing not to harm each other. After a big feast Laban said goodbye to his daughters and grandchildren and returned home.

Jacob then had to face one more dreaded confrontation, that of his brother Esau. When scouts reported to Jacob that Esau was coming to meet him with 400 men, he divided his group into two camps with the thought that if one camp is attacked, the other might have a chance to escape. He also started to send servants in advance with gifts hoping to appease Esau. When they finally met, Jacob was very humble but Esau had apparently had enough time to get over his anger. They greeted each other warmly. Jacob introduced Esau to the family he had acquired since he left home and they parted and went their separate ways.

Jacob went and built shelters for his animals in Sukkoth and eventually moved on to Shechem. While in Shechem, Jacob's daughter Dinah was raped by a local lad whose name coincidently was also Shechem. After the rape, the lad wanted her as his wife. Jacob's sons convinced Shechem and the men of the town that before the marriage could take place, they all had to be circumcised. While the men were still sore, Dinah's brothers slaughtered them all and took their possessions. Fearing possible reprisal from some of the neighboring clans, Jacob moved his group in the direction of Jerusalem. While on the way, Rachel went into labor and gave birth to Benjamin and then died in childbirth. She was buried by the road near Jerusalem.

The focus now shifts to Joseph. Joseph was a precocious and somewhat braggadocios lad. He was a source of irritation to his older brothers. This was in part due to his being Jacob's favorite son and sometimes gave unfavorable reports on their activities to him. The second part was his describing his dreams to them in which he appeared to be in a position of authority over them. One day when Joseph was seventeen, he was sent by Jacob to check on his brothers who were grazing their flocks in a remote location. He was wearing a special colorful coat which had been given to him by Jacob. When they saw him approaching from a distance they plotted to eliminate him. When he was near enough they seized him and threw him a well. A caravan of traders headed for Egypt was passing nearby and one of the brothers said let's not kill him let's sell him to those traders. So he was sold to the traders for a few shekels and carried down to Egypt where he became a slave to the Captain of Pharaoh's guard. The brothers took Joseph's colorful coat and dipped it in the blood of a goat and brought it to Jacob in an attempt to have him believe Joseph had been killed by some wild animal.

Even as a slave, Joseph's leadership capabilities were apparent. He was elevated to the position of head of all the slaves in his master's household. This lush position lasted until his master's wife cast an eye of desire upon him and accused him of improprieties when he refused her advances. He was subsequently arrested and placed in prison. But even in prison he rose to the position of being in charge of all the other prisoners. It was while in prison he encountered two of pharaoh's servants. Both servants had troubling dreams on the same night and did not know their meaning. Joseph interpreted the dreams saying one servant would be restored to his position with Pharaoh and the other would be executed and it happened as he had said.

Two years after Joseph's encounter with the servants, the pharaoh was having dreams that none of his officials or wise men could interpret. The servant who had been restored to Pharaoh's service remembered Joseph and mentioned him to the pharaoh. Pharaoh had him brought in and described his dreams to Joseph. Joseph told Pharaoh that his dreams meant that there would be seven years of bountiful harvest followed by seven years of famine. He further advised that the pharaoh should seek a wise man to be in charge of collecting part of the harvest during the plentiful years and place it in storehouses for the years of famine to come. If Joseph was feathering his own nest the pharaoh fell for it because he said that since Joseph knew all these things he was the wisest man the pharaoh knew. So at age 30, thirteen years after arriving in Egypt as a slave, Joseph was elevated to the position of second in command of all Egypt and put in charge of storing grain during the bountiful harvest to be available during the years of famine. Pharaoh even selected a wife for him from among Egypt's nobility.

When they came, the years of famine were not confined to Egypt. They were being felt in nearby Canaan where Joseph's father Jacob lived with his other sons. Jacob heard somehow that there was grain for sale in Egypt and sent his sons sans Benjamin to Egypt to buy grain. Joseph recognized them but they did not recognize him. Communicating through an interpreter, Joseph accuses his brothers of being spies trying to gather information about their weaknesses for an invading army. They in turn explained that they are all sons of the same father and that their father and youngest brother Benjamin were waiting at home for their return. He put them all in jail for a few days but decided to let them go while keeping one of the brothers in jail. He told them that to prove they were telling the truth, they would have to return with their youngest brother.

Jacob was reluctant to let Benjamin go since he was the only remaining son (or so he thought) of his beloved wife Rachel. After all the grain from the first trip was gone and eminent starvation became apparent, Jacob begrudgingly allowed Benjamin to accompany his brothers back to Egypt.

It was during the second trip that Joseph eventually revealed to his brothers who he was and made preparations to bring his father and all of his brothers families into Egypt. Joseph settled his father and brothers in the best grazing land in all of Egypt, the Nile delta region known as the land of Goshen. Jacob was 130 when he entered Egypt and stayed there until his death some seventeen years later. But in accordance with Jacob's wishes in a promises solicited from Joseph, he was taken back to the family burial place purchased by his grandfather Abraham for internment. Commentary 16 as with Chapter 50 of Genesis ends with the death of Joseph at age 110.

COMMENTARY NO. 1

The Death of Methuselah

Contrary to the tenants of the sciences of Archeology and Anthropology, the first ten patriarchs in Genesis from Adam to Noah each purports to have lived for several centuries (Genesis 5). Each is said to have lived a stated number of years before producing the next offspring in the genealogical sequence then went on to produce other sons and daughters before his eventual demise. While the departure of Enoch, the father of Methuselah and 7th in the sequence of ten (Genesis 5:21) appears to be somewhat unconventional, ("God took him" or "he disappeared"), the others seem quite conventional except for Enoch's son, Methuselah the subject of this commentary.

Methuselah (Genesis 5:25) the 8th in the sequence of the first ten patriarchs is reported to have lived 969 years (Genesis 5:27). When he was 187 years old his son Lemach was born. In Lemach's 182nd year, Lemach's son Noah was born. Lemach died at the age of 777 (Genesis 5:27). By simple arithmetic, it can be shown that the death of Lemach occurred in Noah's 595th year and the death of Methuselah occurred some five years later in Noah's 600th year.

Sometime before his 600th year, God came to Noah and told him to build an ark to house two of every living thing. He told Noah that he was going to destroy all life on earth except for Noah and his wife and their three sons and their wives and all the pairs of creatures he was told to place aboard the ark (Genesis 6:14-20). Noah's sons, Shem Ham and Japheth were born after he was 500 years old (Genesis 5:32). The order of their

1

births although apparently inconsequential is however controversial. This is the subject of Commentary 2. How long after Noah's 500th year his son's births occurred is not given. Perhaps they were born early enough to help in building the ark. At least, they were all born early enough to have acquired wives but apparently no children by the time of the flood.

After the ark was finished and all were aboard, the rain began on the 17th day of the second month of Noah's 600th year (Genesis 7:11). It is not clear whether the reference is to Noah's birth date or some undefined calendar but in any case, as previously determined Methuselah's death occurs during Noah's 600th year and since Noah was only one month and seventeen days into his 600th year at the start of the flood, the question becomes: did Methuselah perish in the flood? Or in typical tabloid fashion one would ask, did Noah allow his poor old grandfather to drown?

Commentary No. 2

The Birth Order of Noah's Sons

After Noah was 500 years old, he had three sons Shem, Ham and Japheth (Genesis 5:32). This is written in such a way to imply the possibility of triplets. Since there is no direct mention of such an occurrence it will not be considered further.

After the flood when Noah had planted a vineyard, made wine, gotten drunk and fallen asleep naked, there is a direct reference to Ham being the youngest son In fact, Ham had told his brothers about their father and they had walked backwards with a robe to cover him. The passage states that when Noah found out what his youngest son had done, he was furious. He went on to place a curse on Ham's son Canaan (Genesis 9:20-25).

While it can be established that both Shem and Japheth are older than Ham is not as easy to tell which of the two of them is older.

It all hinges on the translations of Genesis 10:21 that differ in different versions of the bible. The King James', NRV, The Good News and several other versions start this passage with some variation of "Shem, the elder brother of Japheth…" However, some versions namely, all variations of the NIV, Young's Literal Translation, Darby and some others start this verse with some variation of "Shem, whose older brother was Japheth…" Some versions while choosing one variation in the text acknowledges the second possibility in the footnotes. Since the birth order of the two elder brothers appears to have no impact on the remainder of Genesis, it will not be considered further. In any case, the remainder of Genesis 10:21, the verse where this difference arises, is the beginning of Commentary No. 3.

3

COMMENTARY No. 3

The Hebrews

The full text of Genesis 10:21(NIV) is as follows: "Sons were also born to Shem, whose older brother was Japheth; Shem was the ancestor of all the sons of Eber." In several versions of the bible, either in the foot notes or directly in the text as in the Good News Bible "ancestor of all the sons of Eber" translates into Ancestor of all the Hebrews. The lineage from Shem was –Shem, Arphaxad, Shelah, Eber (Genesis 10:22-24). There is little doubt that the name Hebrew derives from the name Eber, however, the word "Hebrew" is not mentioned in most translations for 5 more generations where it is applied to Eber's great great great grandson Abram(Abraham). This is after Abram's nephew Lot had been captured and carried away by force by a group of five kings. It is stated in Genesis 14:13,"One who had escaped came and reported this to Abram the Hebrew" Abram with 300 of his men joined forces with a group of four opposing kings and was successful in securing Lot's release. The next time it is mention in Genesis is in connection with Abram's great grandson Joseph where he is a servant to Potiphar and is falsely accused by Potiphar's wife of sexual improprieties (Genesis 39:14,17). It is mentioned three more times in Genesis (40:15, 41:12, 43:32) for a total of six times in all.

The previous discussion was introduced to argue the point that it appears that Eber seems to have gotten less than his fair share of accolades in the scheme of things. There is an acknowledged race of people and both a written and verbal means of communicating attributed to him that continues to this day.

"Two sons were born to Eber: One was named Peleg, because in his time the earth was divided; his brother was named Joktan." (Genesis 10:25) Joktan was the father of 13 sons that are named in Genesis 10:26-29. Abram descended from Eber by way of Peleg (Genesis11:16-27) "When Eber had lived 34 years, he became the father of Peleg. And after he became the father of Peleg, Eber lived 430 years and had other sons and daughters. The question one is led to ask here is the following: Are all the descendents of Peleg, Joktan and Eber's other sons and daughters also Hebrews? If so, there seems to be a lot more Hebrews for which to account. Attempts at researching the origin of the Hebrew language, both spoken and written, leads one inevitably to Judaism which arguably should represent only a small subset of the Hebrews.

Jewish tradition has it that Eber refused to help in the building of the Tower of Babel (Genesis 11:1-9), so his language was not confused when the tower fell. And that he and his family alone retained the original human language. After this the language was called Hebrew, named after Eber.

COMMENTARY NO. 4

Abraham, Sarah and Lot

In Genesis 11:26 it states that after Terah lived 70 years he be came the father of Abram, Nahor and Haran. As with the sons of Noah (Commentary 2) no birth order is specified. While Terah was still alive Haran died in Ur of the Chaldeans, in the land of his birth. It can probably be assumed, not conclusively, that Haran was the eldest. At least he is described as the only one with offspring at the time. He is said to have had a son Lot and two other children, Milkah who became the wife of Nahor and the mysterious Iskah, presumably, female, who is never mentioned again. The assumption of Haran being the eldest is somewhat moderated by the fact that Sarai, the wife of Abram was unable to conceive. There has been much speculation that Iskah is another name for Sarai. See Commentary No. 6 where this speculation is disputed and a different speculation is offered.

For reasons not explained, Terah decides to move from his home in Ur of the Chaldeans to Canaan. It is stated that he took with him, Abram and Abram's wife Sarai, and Haran's son Lot. Canaan was almost due west of Ur of the Chaldeans across the Arabian Desert. Apparently to avoid the desert, Terah travels north and got as far as Harran (about 600 miles of approximately an 1100 mile distance to Canaan) and settled there where he continued to live until his death at the age of 205. It does not state that Nahor and Milkah came along with Terah but next time they are mentioned (Genesis 22: 20-23) they are reported to be living in Paddan Aram in close proximity to Harran and have produced 8 sons.

Eventually, the names of Abram and Sarai get changed to Abraham (Genesis 17:5) and Sarah (Genesis 17:15). For the sake of expediency, henceforth, only the latter names will be used.

After some time in Harran, Abraham got the call from God to leave his father's house and continue the journey to Canaan (Genesis 12:1). He was accompanied by his wife Sarah and his nephew Lot. They must have had spent considerable time in Harran because it is stated both he and Lot took with them the possessions and people they had acquired in Harran (Genesis 12:5). Abraham was 75 years old when he left his father's house (Genesis 12:4). We later learn that Sarah is 10 years his junior (Genesis 17:17) and no indications of Lot's age is given but presumably he is younger than Abraham. Contrary to what some have said, most notably Stephen's speech to the Sanhedrin in Acts 7:2-4, it will be assumed that Terah was still alive when Abraham left.

Abraham and his entourage traveled about in Canaan building altars to the Lord while being promised by the Lord that his offspring would inherit the land (Genesis 12:2-9). After some time, there was a famine in the land and Abraham traveled down to Egypt. Sarah was a beautiful woman, and in order to keep the Egyptians from killing him to take her, he allowed them to believe she was his sister (See Commentary No. 9). This ruse allowed his wealth to grow even more until he was exposed and driven out of the country.

Arriving back in Canaan with increased herd sizes, Abraham and Lot found themselves in a situation where the land they were occupying could not support both of them (Genesis 13:6). Herdsmen for Abraham and Herdsmen for Lot began quarrelling with each other (Genesis13:7). Abraham gave Lot the choice to pick any direction and he would go in the opposite direction (Genesis 13:8-9). Lot looked in the direction of the city of Sodom and saw green, well watered grass and chose to go in that direction (Genesis 13:10-11). Lot pitched his tent just outside Sodom. The people of that city he was later to learn were very wicked.

The whole area around which Abraham and Lot settled consisted of a number of small cities or settlements each with its own head man or leader. These leaders are seemingly inappropriately referred to in Genesis 14 as kings. One of the kings, Kedorlaomer of Elam, had been exacting tributes from the kings of Sodom and four other cities for twelve years. In the thirteenth year these cities rebelled (Genesis 14:4). In the fourteenth year Kedorlaomer allied himself with the kings of three other cities who were possibly sharing or would be sharing in his ill-gotten tributes. The four bully kings routed the apparently weaker forces of the five kings and Lot with all of his possessions was captured and carried away in the process (Genesis 14:8-12).

When Abraham heard that Lot had been captured, he took the 318 men in his service and allied himself with Mamre the Amorite and Mamre's two brothers Eshkol and Aner and went after Kedorlaomer and his allies. They rescued Lot and returned with all the possessions they had taken (Genesis 14:13-16).

At this point things get really mysterious. On returning from battle Abraham is met by Bera king of Sodom (Genesis 14:17). Then Melchizedek king of Salem brought out bread and wine. He was priest of God Most High, and he blessed Abraham. In return, Abraham gives him a tenth of all the reclaimed possessions (Genesis 14:18-20). Why? Who was this mysterious priest that Abraham apparently instantly recognized the importance of and would grant him such tribute and respect? Melchizedek is mentioned once more in Psalms 110:4 with the line "You are a priest forever, in the order of Melchizedek." There are also references to Melchizedek in Hebrews chapters 5 and 7 where Christ is referred to as a priest in the order of Melchizedek.

One can only speculate that anyone living in the time and culture of Abraham would recognize the name and importance of Melchizedek. There is not enough information, however, to accord such recognition to our culture and time.

COMMENTARY NO. 5

Abraham, Ishmael and Isaac

Sometime after the rescue of Lot (Commentary No. 4), God appeared to Abraham in a dream in which he made a covenant with him and promised him metaphorically that his descendants would be as numerous as the stars in the sky. He even explained to him that his descendants would be enslaved in a foreign land for 400 years and he would then bring them out to take the land in which Abraham resided (Genesis 15:12-16). Abraham made the point that he currently had no heirs from which the descendants would come.

Sarah, apparently sensing the strain that Abraham was under and possibly blaming her own infertility as part of the problem, offers her much younger Egyptian slave Hagar to Abraham as a wife (Genesis 16:1-2). Abraham consented and Hagar became pregnant. Once pregnant, Hagar began to despise and mock her mistress and Sarah placed the blame for the deteriorating situation on Abraham. Abraham said she is your slave, do with her as you will. Then Sarah began treating Hagar so harshly, that she ran away (Genesis 16:6). But God encountered Hagar in the wilderness and told her to go back and submit to her mistress for she carried within her the seed to a great nation (Genesis 16:9-14). She returned to Sarah and eventually gave birth to a son and named him Ishmael. Abraham was 86 years old at the birth of Ishmael (Genesis 16:15).

Ishmael grew up and in Ismael's thirteenth year, Abraham was visited by God with the covenant of circumcision. God told Abraham that henceforth all males in his household whether family or servants would have to be circumcised. Abraham was 99 years old when he and Ishmael and all male members of his household were circumcised (Genesis 17:23-27).

Shortly after the circumcision, Abraham is sitting at the entrance of his tent in the heat of the day and sees three strangers approaching.

In a manner of hospitality typical to the area, Abraham bows to the three strangers and offers to allow them to wash their feet and sets about having a meal prepared for them (Genesis 18:1-5). It quickly becomes apparent that the strangers are not ordinary men. They are in fact the Lord and two angels. They tell Abraham that the descendants that he had been promised would inherit the land would not be from Ishmael but would be from a son born to Sarah within a year. Sarah overhears this and laughs thinking I am to have a child at age ninety. One of the strangers asked, why did Sarah laugh? She pretended that she hadn't laughed but the stranger said you did laugh (Genesis 18:10-15).

Next the conversation turned to the reports the Lord had been getting about the wicked nature of the town of Sodom. He had decided to send the two angels down to check it out and declared if it was as bad as the reports he would destroy it. Apparently, realizing his nephew Lot was in the vicinity, Abraham starts pleading with the Lord to spare Sodom. He starts by asking if 50 righteous people are found there would the city be spared. When the answer was in the affirmative, he started lowering the ante at first five then ten people at a time until he was down to only ten righteous people the city would be spared (Genesis 18:16-32). Apparently, the two angels didn't find ten righteous people (Commentary No. 6) because the next morning, Abraham looked down and saw dense smoke coming from the direction of Sodom.

As promised, a year after the visit of the three Sarah gave birth to Isaac (Genesis 21:2). The boy grew and at the feast that was given when he was weaned, the conflict was reignited between Sarah and Hagar. Sarah saw Ishmael mocking Isaac and she told Abraham," send that woman and her son away from here, he will never share an inheritance with my son" (Genesis 21:8-10). Abraham reluctantly complied because Ishmael was also his son. He helped them pack up and sent them away and Ishmael grew up away from Abraham and Isaac (Genesis 21:11-14).

Next the Lord imposed a test on Abraham's faithfulness. He told Abraham to take his son Isaac and sacrifice him on the altar. Abraham, without hesitation, took Isaac up on a mountain, built an altar, bound his son up and drew his knife to sacrifice him when an angel of the Lord said "do not harm the boy this is a test of your faithfulness to the Lord." Abraham found a ram stuck in a thicket nearby and used it for the sacrifice instead (Genesis 22:1-13).

A great deal is made of Abraham and Sarah not having children until such an advanced age. Perhaps rightly so in the case of Sarah giving birth to Isaac at age ninety. However, she lived another thirty seven years after the birth of Isaac to age 127 (Genesis 23:1). Even more remarkable is that after the death of Sarah, Abraham took another wife named Keturah and had six more sons (Genesis 25:1-2). One of those sons, named Midian was the apparent ancestor of Jethro the Midianite, father-in-law of Moses some 400 to 500 years later. Abraham lived to be 175 years old and his sons Ishmael and Isaac buried him (Genesis 25:7-10). Apparently, there had been reconciliation between them.

Commentary No. 6

Lot's Fate and Legacy

While the Lord and two angels were visiting with Abraham to inform him of the coming birth of Isaac by his wife Sarah, he broached the wicked nature of the town of Sodom and that he might be beholden to destroy it. So the two angels were dispatched to Sodom to check it out. Then Abraham, knowing of Lot's presence in the vicinity of Sodom started to plea with the Lord for circumstances in which Sodom might be spared. See Commentary No. 5.

Upon arriving at the city of Sodom, the two angels encounter Lot at the city gate. With hospitality common for the time, Lot invites them to his place to spend the night (Genesis 19:1-3). Then all the men of the city, both young and old surrounded the house and shouted, "Where are the two men that came to your house? Bring them out so we can have sex with them" (Genesis 19:4-5). Lot went outside closed the door behind him with the two angels inside. Lot's next move was totally incomprehensible. He told the men that he had two virgin daughters and told them to take his daughters and do with them as they will but to leave the two visitors alone (Genesis 19:6-8). The men vehemently rejected that proposal and told Lot that he was a foreigner among them and that they would treat him worse than the visitors. The men rushed the door to Lot's house and the Angels reached out and pulled Lot inside. At the same time, they blinded the men near the door so that they could not find it (Genesis 19:9-11).

The Angeles told Lot that the city was going to be destroyed and to take his family and head for the mountains. But Lot protested that the mountains were too far. He looked in the direction of the small town of Zoar and said he could make that far. The angels agreed to spare the town of Zoar and told Lot to hurry toward it and don't look back but Lot's wife looked back and was turned into a pillar of salt. The Lord rained down burning sulfur destroying Sodom and Gomorrah and all the cities of the plains except Zoar and Lot and his two daughters were able arrive there safely (Genesis 19:15-26).

Later, Lot and his daughters moved from Zoar to the mountains and lived in a cave. The story is that the daughters realizing that there were no men around to give them children to preserve their legacy decided to get their father drunk with wine and have sex with him. They did so and both got pregnant. The elder daughter gave birth to a son and named him Moab. He is the ancestor of the Moabites. The younger daughter also bore a son and named him Ben-Ammi. He is the ancestor of the Ammonites (Genesis 19:30-38). Both of these tribes were destined for future confrontations with the descendants of Abraham

How or when Lot acquired a wife is not explained. There is no mention of a wife prior to the arrival of the two angels in Sodom. Yet at that time he has a wife and two daughters old enough to be married. Since Abraham left his father's house at age 75 and was visited by the Lord and two angels at age 99 it had been 24 years since they left Terah's house. Did Lot take a Canaanite wife or was he already married when they left Terah's house? In either case he would have to have been married long enough to have produced two daughters old enough to be married.

This introduces another possible solution for "Who was Ishka? The persistent assertion that Sarah(Sarai) and Ishka are the same person is adequately dismissed by Abraham himself when he declared that she was indeed his sister, the daughter of his father but of a different mother (Genesis 20:12). Isn't it possible that the same situations entails here? Lot and Ishka were siblings (Genesis 11:29) and since men of the time often had multiple wives and/or concubines, the same situation as with Abraham and Sarah could be applicable.

COMMENTARY NO. 7

Isaac and Rebeka

About three years after the death of Sarah, Abraham sent his senior servant back to the family of his brother Nahor to seek a wife for Isaac because he did not want him to marry a Canaanite woman (Genesis 24:1-4). Abraham's servant encounters the family of Bethuel; son of Nahor. Bethuel had a son named Laban and a daughter named Rebeka. With some amount of negotiating with the family and the consent of Rebeka herself, she returns with the servant to become the wife of Isaac (Genesis 24: 15-59). Apparently they were quite well-to do because she was sent with her own personal nurse.

Rebeka's brother Laban, probably an older brother, seems to have an undue influence in family matters. Most of the negotiating is done by Laban and his mother with the father Betheul having little to say. One quickly develops an air of greed and mistrust for Laban which is amply borne out in his later encounters with Rebeka's son Jacob (Commentary No. 10).

Isaac was 40 years old (Genesis 25:20) when he took Rebeka to be his wife. There is no reference to the actual age of Rebeka but she was still a virgin so a conjecture would place her age at around 15 or 16 years old. The couple remains childless for 20 years until they become pregnant with twin sons (Genesis 25:23). The boys were quite different. The firstborn was red and hairy and was given the name Esau which means hairy. The second born, on the other hand, was smooth and he came out grasping the heel of the first born. He was given the name Jacob which means one who grasps by the heel it is also a Hebrew idiom for one who takes advantage or deceives

(Genesis 25:24-26). The two boys grew up with quite a different out look on life. Esau was an outdoors and hunter type while Jacob preferred hanging around the tents (Genesis 25:27).

Esau being the firstborn was entitled to inheritance from his father by birthright. One day Esau came from hunting very famished and Jacob had prepared some lentil soup. Esau said give some of that "red stuff" referring to the lentil soup. Jacob said I will trade you some soup for your birthright. Esau agreed saying what good is a birthright to me when I am starving (Genesis 25:29-34). There is an article on the internet that suggests that this incident occurred coincident with the death of Abraham and the lentil soup had been prepared for Isaac because lentil soup is the Jewish food of mourning. If this is true, the boys would have been around fifteen years old at the time.

Isaac, Rebeka and the boys were the existential dysfunctional family. Isaac preferred Esau the outdoors hunter type while Rebeka favored the stay at home Jacob. At age 40 Esau marries two Canaanite women much to the displeasure of both Isaac and Rebeka (Genesis 26:34).

Sometime later, Isaac has gotten old and nearly blind and feels that his remaining days are few. He tells Esau to take his bow and go out and catch some wild game and prepare a meal for him so he can give him his blessing (Genesis 27:1-4). Rebeka overhears the conversation and schemes to have the blessing delivered to Jacob (Genesis 27:5-7). She has Jacob bring two young goats to prepare a meal for Isaac and had him dress in Esau's clothes. When Jacob complained that he was not hairy like Esau, she had him put goat skin over his arms (Genesis 27:11-17). Rebeka prepares the meal for Jacob to take to his father. When Jacob brought the meal to Isaac, he was somewhat suspicious of the voice but t because of the smell of Esau clothes and the feel of his hairy arms he relented and gave his blessing (Genesis 25:18-29).

When Esau come back from his hunt and prepared and brought a meal to Isaac in anticipation of his blessing, Isaac inquired as to whom he had just given his blessing (Genesis 27:31-31). Esau, realizing what had happened, asked Isaac if he also had a blessing for him. When Isaac said he only had one blessing, Esau became so angry and said "isn't he rightly named Jacob he has taken advantage of me twice, first he stole my birthright and now he has taken my blessing." He then said the time for mourning for my father is near and when that is done, I will kill Jacob (Genesis 27:41). Rebeka fearing for Jacobs's life told him to run away to her brother Laban in Paddan Aram near Harran until Esau's anger was abated (Genesis 27:42-45). She also enlisted Isaac in the send off through their mutual dislike for Esau's Canaanite wives by having him bless Jacob and send him to seek a wife among Laban's family (Genesis 27:46-28:1-5). Esau, realizing how much his parents disliked his Canaanite wives went out and took another wife from the daughters of his uncle Ishmael (Genesis 28:8-9). The confusion about the names of Esau's wives is the subject of Commentary No. 8.

The irony in this story is the apparent stressing of the eminent demise of Jacob when it can be estimated from the time tags to be around 120 years old. The twins who are often portrayed in entertainment media as quarreling teenagers were about sixty years old. But Isaac was still alive when Jacob returned from living with Laban some twenty years or so later and went on to live to the age of 180 (Genesis 35:28). There is no record of how long Rebeka lived but in Jacob's statement in Genesis 49:22 she is buried in the family grave along with Isaac. There is a record of Rebeka's nurse Deborah dying (Gen 35:8) while traveling with Jacob's family to Bethel after the rape of Dinah (Commentary No. 12). Whether this is the same nurse that arrived with Rebeka from Padaan Aram and how she comes to be traveling with Jacob is not given.

Commentary No. 8

Esau's Wives

One of the most obvious mismatches in the book Genesis is in the naming of Esau's wives. In Genesis 26 it is asserted when Esau was forty years old, he married Judith daughter of Beeri the Hittite, and also Basemath daughter of Elon the Hittite. It further states that they were a source of grief to Isaac and Rebecca. In Genesis 28 when Esau learned that Isaac had blessed Jacob and had sent him to Paddan Aram to take a wife from there, and that when he blessed him he commanded him, "Do not marry a Canaanite woman," and that Jacob had obeyed his father and mother and had gone to Paddan Aram.

Esau realizing how displeasing the Canaanite women were to his father Isaac; went to his uncle Ishmael and married his daughter Mahalath, the sister of Nebaioth, in addition to the wives he already had.

In Genesis 36 it states that Esau took his wives from the women of Canaan: Adah daughter of Elon the Hittite, and Oholibamah daughter of Anah and granddaughter of Zibeon the Hivite— also Basemath daughter of Ishmael and sister of Nebaioth.

To recap,

Esau's original Hittite wives in Genesis 26

Basemath (daughter of Elon the Hittite)

Judith (daughter of Beeri the Hittite)

Esau then marries in Genesis 28

Mahalath (daughter of Ishmael son of Abraham, sister of Nebaioth)

Esau's wives in Genesis 36

Adah (daughter of Elon the Hittite)

Oholibamah (daughter of Anah and granddaughter of Zibeon the Hivite)

Basemath (daughter of Ishmael son of Abraham, sister of Nebaioth)

It was claimed in an internet article that the name Basemath is a term of endearment and could have easily been assigned to another wife. Even if that is the case, it does not explain the other wives name changes and also in one case the assignment of a different father-in-law as well.

COMMENTARY No. 9

Say to Them, You are My Sister.

The ruse to pass off a wife as the husband's sister is used three times in the book of Genesis. It is used twice by Abraham and once by Isaac. Some of the circumstances surrounding the second attempt by Abraham strains credulity.

The first time for Abraham seems plausible. The first time it occurs is in Genesis 12 where the 75 year old Abraham had recently departed his father's house and there was a famine in the land and Abraham took his beautiful 65 year old wife down to Egypt. Abraham told Sarah it would go well with him if she say she was his sister. The Pharaoh took Sarah as his own and lavished Abraham with gifts. It was with disastrous results for the Pharaoh, however, in the form of serious diseases being inflicted on his entire household (Genesis 12:17). He admonished Abraham for not saying Sarah was his wife and said "take your wife and go" (Genesis 12:18-20)

The second time Abraham is said to have used this ruse was in Genesis 20. This is also the chapter where he says she really is my sister, daughter of my father but of a different mother (Genesis 20:12). The problem with the credulity of this occurrence was it is said to have happened after so many defining events. First there had been the separation of Lot and his abduction and his subsequent recovery by Abraham. Next there had been the covenant with Abraham where he was promised that his descendants would inherit the land. Then there was the birth of Abraham's son Ishmael by Hagar, Sarah's Egyptian slave followed thirteen years later by the covenant of circumcision. Then last but not least, there had been the three visitors who promised a 99 year old Abraham that a son would be born to him by his wife Sarah within a year and that was then followed by the complete destruction of Sodom and Gomorrah.

One can readily observe the uncanny similarities of Abraham's second use of the ruse (Genesis 20) with the one in which Isaac is said to have Rebecca say he was her brother (Genesis 26). Isaac's event would have occurred at least 75 years later after the death of Abraham at age 175. In each case, the person to placate was named Abimilek, king of the Phillistines at Gerar and in each case the protagonist became wealthier because of the encounter. And also, in each case there was a dispute over wells between the protagonist and the herders of Gerar. Although it is possible King Abimilek of Abraham's time could have had a descendent in Isaac's time with the same name it is probably not likely that each would have shown up with a commander of his forces named Phicol (Genesis 21:22 and Genesis 26:26).

It certainly seems plausible that some historian, using either oral or written tradition could have intermixed and confused the deeds of the two patriarchs. The odds are further bolstered in favor Isaac because of the following. While Rebecca, although a middle aged woman at that time could have still looked good enough to attract attention. Sarah on the other hand, would have been approaching ninety and quite possibly pregnant with Isaac and could hardly expected to have been the object of anyone's desire except Abraham's.

COMMENTARY No. 10

Jacob and Laban

After receiving Isaacs blessing and being told to seek a wife from the daughters of his uncle Laban, Jacob left his father's house in Beersheba bound for Paddan Aram near Haran (Genesis 28:5). When he reached a certain place, he stopped for the night and took one of the stones there and placed it under his head for a pillow. While sleeping, he had a dream in which he saw a ladder reaching from the earth up into heaven. Angels were ascending and descending the ladder and the Lord God stood at the top of it. In his dream, the Lord spoke to saying he was the God of Abraham and Isaac and made him the promise formerly made to Abraham of his descendants occupying the land on which he rested (Genesis 28:10-15). When he awakened he was afraid and said to himself, surely God must be in this place. He set up the rock which he had used as a pillow and poured oil on it and named the place Bethel which means House of God. He promised the Lord that if he would be with him and provide for him in all his travels and bring him safely back to his father's house, he would give him a tenth of all he acquired (Genesis 28:18-22).

Jacob then continued on his journey. As he came near Harran, he saw three flocks of sheep with their shepherds resting near a well of water that was covered by a large stone. He asked the shepherds where they were from. They replied that they were from Haran. He then asked if they knew Laban the grandson of Nahor. They replied that they did and added that the person approaching was Laban's daughter Rachel with Laban's flock (Genesis 29:1-6).

He then admonishes the shepherds for having their flocks lay around in the middle of the day when they could be out grazing. They explained that they had to wait for all the flocks to gather before rolling away the stone from the well so they could all be watered at the same time. As Rachel approached the well, he acted either to assert his feeling as to the ridiculous nature of the rules by which they acted or to appear macho in front of his pretty young cousin by rolling away the stone so the flock herded by Rachel could be watered. He emotionally explained to Rachel who he was and she ran to tell her father Laban. Laban came out to greet Jacob and took him to his house (Genesis 29:7-14).

This begins a twenty year encounter where Laban, the epitome of avarice does all he can to enrich himself through extorting free labor from Jacob. But what Laban failed to understand is that he was dealing with the deceptive heel grasper.

Apparently with many family matters to exchange, Jacob had spent a month with Laban helping out with the chores etc. when Laban tells Jacob just because you are family you shouldn't have to work for me for free. Jacob who apparently for all month had been eying the beautiful young Rachel proposed to Laban to work for him for seven years to have Rachel as a wife. Laban agrees and the seven years pass quickly for Jacob (Genesis 29:18-20).

But Laban had two daughters Rachel was the younger daughter the elder was named Leah (Genesis 29:16). Since Rachel was considered old enough to marry, she must have been at least in her mid teens say fifteen or sixteen. By all accounts, Rachel was the prettier of the two. There was something unusual probably even unexplainable about Leah's eyes[1].

At the end of the seven years, Rachel is probably in her early to middle twenties and Leah is possibly in middle to late twenties. Jacob tells Laban to let me have my wife so that I may consummate my marriage. This starts a week long celebration called the bridal week. After an apparent night of celebration he awakens in the morning and finds he has consummated his marriage with Leah (Genesis 29:21-24). It is not certain how Laban pulled this off. Perhaps he told Leah not to speak or to try and sound like Rachel if she did. And plying Jacob with a few extra glasses of wine might have helped. In any case, when the morning came, Jacob realized he had been tricked. When he asked Laban "why"? Laban replied that in our country it is not the custom to have the younger daughter marry before the elder. But he immediately seized upon the opportunity to get more free labor out of Jacob telling him to let Leah finish her bridal week he could then also have Rachel for a wife for another seven year of labor (Genesis 29:25-27). Jacob's love for Rachel was strong enough that he agreed (Genesis 29:28-30). It is not certain if Rachel ever got her bridal week or if she had share the bridal week the same as she had to share her husband with Leah. Laban was well off enough to supply each of his daughters with their own personal servants. Rachel received Bilhah as her servant and Leah received zilpah. Jacob loved Rachel more than Leah but Leah was fertile. Leah got pregnant right away and started having babies. The first born was Reuben who was followed in succession by Simeon, Levi and Judah (Genesis 29:31-35).

Rachel, meanwhile, became quite distraught and told Jacob "give me children or I will die." Jacob became angry with her and said "am I in the place of God who has kept you from having children?" (Genesis 30:1-2) Rachel then decided to try a practice acceptable at the time which had been used by Jacob's grandmother Sarah (Commentary No. 4) with dire consequences of offering her servant to her husband as a wife and since the servant was hers the children would also be hers. She gave Bilhah to Jacob. Bilhah conceived and gave birth to Dan. She conceived again and gave birth to Naphtali (Genesis 30:3-8). Leah, perhaps still feeling unloved possible thinks Rachel is catching up with her gives her servant Zilpah to Jacob as a wife. Zilpah conceived and gave birth to Gad. She conceived again and gave birth to Asher (Genesis 30:9-13)

During wheat harvest, Reuben went out in the field and found some mandrakes and brought them to his mother Leah. Mandrakes were considered as a sort of aphrodisiac[2] and it was also believed to increase the fertility in women. Rachel said to Leah, "Please give me some of your son's Mandrakes." But she said to Rachel, "Wasn't it enough that you took away my husband? Will you take my son's mandrakes also?" Rachel said, "very well, he can stay with you tonight in return for your son's mandrakes." So when Jacob came in from the fields that evening, Leah went out to meet him. She said, "You must sleep with me tonight, I have hired you with my son's mandrakes." So he slept with her that night (Genesis 30:14-16).

Leah's fertility was restored and she gave birth to a fifth son and named him Issachar. She conceived again and gave birth to a sixth son and named him Zebulun. Sometime later she gave birth to a daughter which she gave the name of Dinah (Genesis 30:17-21). Then finally, Rachel conceives and gives birth to a son which is given the name Joseph (Genesis 30:22-24). Joseph is destined to be a key player in the family's developing dynamics.

Before proceeding, it is well to ponder how at least the first eleven of Jacob's twelve children could be born sequentially in seven years. Especially, since seven of the twelve came from one mother and there was a hiatus between her first four and the last three. It is assumed here and in other commentaries that although Joseph was born after Dinah they could have been close to the same age. But gestation time alone, with no recovery time, for the first eleven sequential births is 99 months. This exceeds seven years by a year three months. There would have had to be some overlap in gestation. Or, perhaps, although not mentioned, there could have been one or more incidences of multiple births. Multiple births would still allow preservation of the sequential birth order. These are just suggestions, not definitive solutions. The real underlying circumstances will no doubt always remain a mystery.

Continuing on, after the birth of Joseph, Jacob tells Laban that it is time for him to put something together for his own family. Both Jacob and Laban agree that during the fourteen years which Jacob had been helping him that Laban had prospered greatly. Of course, Laban tells Jacob that he hoped that he would stay and continue helping him But Jacob says he would like to return to the home of his father Isaac with his wives and children. Laban then asks Jacob how he could reward him for his years of service (Genesis 30:25-30). He said don't give me anything. I will continue to serve you for a while and take as my reward all the stripped, speckled and spotted of the herds of goats and sheep. Laban agrees while no doubt immediately starting to scheme how to circumvent the whole operation (Genesis 30:31-34).

The first thing Laban did is to go through all his herds and pull out all of his stripped, spotted and speckled animals and turned them over to his sons to put a three days distance between them and Jacob (Genesis 30:35-36). Prior to this point in the narrative, there had not been any mention of Laban's sons. Laban's apparently lack of knowledge of simple genetics possibly led him to believe that he could eliminate or at least slow the production of spotted and speckled animals by eliminating spotted and speckled parent animals. But Jacob the deceitful heel grasper decides on a scheme of his own which was no doubt equally void of any genetic considerations. Jacob knew that when the female animals were in heat, mating often took place at the watering troughs. So Jacob took branches from the poplar, almond and planar trees and carved them so that the white was showing through the bark and he placed them in front of the troughs by the mating animals. He restricted this practice to the healthier animals and omitted it from the more feeble animals. Jacob apparently believed that this practice would result in production of more stripped, spotted and speckled healthy animals (Genesis 30:37-42). Whether this scheme actually worked or if probability was slanted in his favor or there was divine intervention is not known. But, over the next few years Jacob's herds grew tremendously and he became quite wealthy and acquired many servants, camels and donkeys as well (Genesis 30:43). Apparently, Laban's herds did not fare nearly as well.

Jacob, after being with Laban for about twenty years now, noticed that Laban's attitude toward him had changed and he heard that Laban's sons were complaining that his wealth was derived from their fathers flock. Jacob apparently decided that the best time to leave was when Laban was not anywhere around. When Laban was away shearing sheep, Jacob called his wives Leah and Rachel out into the field and made known his intentions to them and asked if they would be willing to go. They answered "we have no inheritance with our father he has essentially sold us." Rachel must have had some struggles between her beliefs in the God of Jacob and the idol gods of her father. Perhaps it was of long protracted time to conceive a child or maybe she just wanted to hedge her bets. In any case, she stole her father's household idols and stuffed them into her camel saddlebags in preparation for the journey. So Jacob and his wives and twelve children, with his vast herd of stripped, spotted and speckled goats and sheep, pack animals and servants (Genesis 31:1-21).

Jacob was gone three days before Laban found out. Laban decided to pursue him and caught up with him in seven days in the hills of Gilead. That night Laban had a dream in which God told him to say nothing either good or bad to Jacob. That did not stop Laban from verbally ranting at Jacob. He tells Jacob that this is a bad thing he had done running off with his daughters like prisoners of war. He says he didn't get to kiss them and his grandchildren goodbye and he could have sent them off with a big celebration. He ends his rant by asking Jacob, "Why did you steal my household gods?"(Genesis 31:22-30)

Jacob answered that he thought Laban would take his wives from by force and send him away with nothing. And not knowing that Rachel had taken Laban's gods, search among us for your gods and anyone found with them will not live. There are two things worthy of comment here. First the prescribed punishment seems very harsh for the crime and second it seems unusual that the head of a family unit would have the power to pass a sentence of death to anyone in the unit. First Laban searched the tents of the two servants and the Leah's tent. Then he goes into Rachel tent where Rachel apologizes for not standing and explaining that she was having her period. Actually she was sitting on her saddlebags containing Laban's household gods (Genesis 31:31-35).

Laban having found nothing, it became time for Jacob to vent his anger. He complained that he had worked for Laban for twenty years, burning up in the daytime and freezing at night. He explained how he had absorbed losses of animal miscarrying or be torn up by wild animals and kept them from Laban. And yet, Laban had changed his wages ten times. Then Laban in Genesis 31:43 indicates that he still felt that he was being taking advantage of by Jacob. He states "the women are my daughters, the children are my children and the flocks are my flocks. All you see is mine." And yet he felt because of the admonishment by God in his dream he was powerless to do anything about it (Genesis 31:36-43).

Jacob and Laban set up a stone as a pillar and gathered more stones and piled them into a heap. Then they made a covenant in which they mutually agreed that neither would pass beyond the pillar and heap to harm each other. Jacob then sacrificed an animal and they all participated in a big feast. The next morning Laban kissed his daughters and grandchildren goodbye and started toward home (Genesis 31:44-55). Jacob prepared to continue his journey toward his father's home in Canaan with an even bigger foe to encounter, his brother Esau who had sworn to kill him.

Footnotes:

1. The controversy about Leah's eyes (Genesis 29:17) was looked at over several versions of the bible thanks to Biblegateway.com. The descriptions varied from not so good to complementary. In almost every case, either in a footnote or the text itself, there would be an alternative description which was sometimes completely contradictory to the first. Some of the references were weak eyes, tender eyes, and delicate eyes, blear eyed, bleary eyed, blurry eyed, her eyes didn't sparkle, and there was no brightness in her eyes. She was also described as having ordinary eyes, nice eyes, gentle eyes, lovely eyes and attractive eyes. Two footnotes worthy of noting was one, that the meaning of the Hebrew word describing Leah's eyes was uncertain and another said it was possibly a courteous way of saying she was not very nice looking. But even those versions that described Leah's eyes as complementary went on to describe Rachel as the preferred choice. One in particular said Leah's eyes were lovely but Rachel's eyes were lovelier and she had a beautiful figure.

   However the harshest criticism of all came from the Luther Bible which when translated from German said "Leah had a stupid face but Rachel was beautiful and lovely."

2. In some versions of the bible, the word Mandrakes is used in these passages without any further explanation. Other versions offer footnotes describing mandrakes as a plant with sexual powers or a source of fertility in women. Still others change the text from mandrakes to terms such as erotic herbs, love flowers, or love apples.

COMMENTARY No. 11

Jacob Meets Esau

Jacob sent messengers ahead to Esau in Edom in the land of Seir.

He said to tell him that he had been staying with Laban until now (Genesis 32:1-5).

The messengers returned and said Esau was coming to meet Jacob and that he had 400 men with him. Jacob divided his household along with his flocks and herds into two groups. He thought that if Esau attacked one group, the other perhaps the other could escape (Genesis 32:7-8).

Then Jacob started praying and reminding God of his promise to make his descendants as plentiful as the grains of sand of the sea. He complained that Esau would probably come and kill him and all his wives and children (Genesis 32:9-12).

He stayed there for the night and took a couple hundred sheep, a couple hundred goats and a smattering of camels and donkeys and divided them into several small herds. He placed a servant with each herd and sent the herds out one by one as gifts to Esau. He instructed each servant in turn that when he met Esau and he asked whose servant are you and where are you going with this herd of animals you are to say "they are from your servant Jacob. They are a gift sent to my lord Esau and he is coming behind us." Jacob stayed there for the night in camp. But during the night he got up and wakened his two wives and, their two servants and his twelve children and sent them across the Jordan River at the Jabbok ford with all his possessions and returned again to the camp where he was all alone (Genesis 32:13-19).

A man wrestled with Jacob until dawn. When the man saw that he could not win, he struck Jacob on the thigh and knocked his hip bone out of its socket. The man said let me go for it is daybreak. Jacob said, "I will not let you go unless you bless me." "What is your name?" the man asked. "Jacob", he answered. "It is not Jacob any more!" the man told him. It is Israel – one who has power with God." What is your name? Jacob asked. No, you mustn't ask the man said and blessed him there. Jacob named the place "Peniel" ("The Face of God"), for he said, "I have seen God face to face yet my life was spared." The sun came up and he started on and he was limping because of his hip. (That is why even today the people of Israel do not eat meat from near the hip, in memory of what happened that night (Genesis 32:22-32).

It is interesting to note that his first encounter with God and angels ascending and descending a ladder is attributed to a dream yet in this case where he was under great stress from the approaching Esau that this would be treated as an actual occurrence. One would think he was in prime condition for a hideous nightmare. There are other weaknesses too, for instance, what would keep a supernatural being from being able to break loose from him? It is also significant that this renaming of Jacob to Israel which occurs in this passage (Genesis 32:27) is repeated much later in time (Genesis 35:9) just prior to the birth of Benjamin as if it had not already occurred.

Jacob looked and saw Esau with his 400 men drawing near and he divided his family into groups. He put the two servants and their children first. Leah and her children were next and then Rachel and Joseph. Jacob went ahead of them. This brings to light that children were regarded according to their birth status or the father's affection for the mother. You could almost imagine one child taunting another with "your mother is my mother's servant." The one noble thing which can be attributed to Jacob is he went ahead of all of them. As Jacob approached his brother Esau he bowed to the ground seven times (Genesis 33:1-7).

When Esau saw Jacob he ran and hugged and kissed him and they both cried. Then Esau asked "who are all these people with you?" Jacob answered,

"These are children that God has given me. First the two servants and their children came and bowed before Esau. Next Leah and her children came and bowed before Esau. Finally Rachel and Joseph came and Bowed before Esau. Then Esau asked, "Who were all those people I saw coming here and what were all the animals for?" Jacob replied, "They were a gift for you so that you might accept me." Esau said, "I don't need them, I have plenty" but because Jacob insisted, Esau accepted them (Genesis 33:8-11).

Then Esau said "Now you can continue your journey and I will accompany you." But Jacob said, "My children are small and some of my animals are nursing and I can not move them very fast. You go on ahead and we will catch up with you in Seir." Then Esau offered to leave some men to help but Jacob declined the offer (Genesis 33:12-15). So on that day Esau started on his trip back to Seir. But Jacob turned and went to Sukkoth where he built a house for himself and shelters for his animals (Genesis 33:16). It is possible that Jacob thought that given time, Esau might start remembering past grudges that were lost in the moment. There is no way to determine how long he remained in Sukkoth but from there he moved on to Shechem. He bought land within sight of the city from the sons of Hamor the Hivite ruler of the area and the father of Shechem the most honored of his family (Genesis 33:18-19).

Many years later on the occasion of Isaac's death at age of 180 Jacob and Esau again came together to bury him (Genesis 35:27-29). Isaac's death approximately coincides in time with Joseph's rise to power in Egypt. But, of course, Jacob did not know that Joseph was still alive at the time.

Commentary No. 12

The Rape of Dinah

After Jacob reconciled with Esau upon arriving back in Caanan from Paddan Aram, Esau departed for Seir and Jacob built shelter for his animals and settled in Sukkoth (Genesis 33:16). From there he moved on to Shechem. He bought land within sight of the city from the sons of Hamor the Hivite ruler of the area and father Shechem the most honored of his family (Genesis 33:18-19). There is no way to determine how long he remained in Sukkoth before moving on to Shechem but Dinah must have been around six years old when they left Paddan Aram.

One can only speculate whether the name of the city was applied in retrospect after considering what happened next. One day Dinah, seventh child of Leah, and Jacob's only daughter went out to visit with the women of the land. When Shechem saw her he took her and raped her (Genesis 34:1-2). To consider Shechem's action to be limited to rape and not child molestation, it will be assumed that Dinah was at least middle teens by this time. But it was still prior to the birth of Benjamin and Joseph being sold into slavery at age seventeen.

Shechem subsequently fell madly in love with Dinah and asked Hamor to get the girl for his wife (Genesis 34:3-4). Jacob heard of it but did nothing until his sons came in from the field. When her brothers heard of it they were furious (Genesis 34:5-6).

Hamor approached Jacob with the proposal of intermarriage between their tribes. Shechem offered to Dinah's father and brothers "let me find favor in your eyes and I will give whatever you ask" (Genesis 34:11-12). Dinah's brothers answered deceitfully to Shechem, we can not allow our sister to marry someone who is uncircumcised, that would be a disgrace to us. If you agree to become circumcised we would allow the intermarriage (Genesis 34:13-17). Shechem agreed right away and was circumcised (Genesis 34:18-19)d. Then Hamor called all the men of Shechem to the gate of the city and made the proposal to them and they all agreed (Genesis 34:20-24).

While the men were still sore and recovering Dinah's brothers Simeon and Levi, sons of Leah, took their swords and killed all the men of the city and made off with all their livestock, wealth and women and children (Genesis 34:25-29). Jacob fearing reprisal from neighboring tribes since they were the strangers in the land leaves the area to travel to Bethel (Genesis 34:30).

It is no doubt that what Shechem did was despicable but is it any more so than the acts of Simeon and Levi. In doing what they did, they no doubt condemned Dinah to a life of spinsterhood since she was then a used woman. Instead, she could have been united with a man who truly loved her. Also, what did the brothers do with the women and children they abducted? Were they made slaves or concubines? Is this any less than what happened to Dinah? And also, how much loyalty could they expect from the women and children they captured after having killed all their loved ones?

COMMENTARY NO. 13

The Death of Rachel and Birth of Benjamin

One of the purposes of this commentary among other things is to establish some semblance of the age difference between Benjamin and his other siblings. This age difference becomes important in some other commentaries.

Dinah followed by Joseph were the last born of Jacob in Paddan Aram. They were both born toward the end of or possibly just after the second seven year period of labor that Jacob provided to Laban for Marrying Leah and Rachel. It is likely they were near the same age with Dinah being slightly the eldest. Since Jacob spent an additional six years building up his spotted and speckled flocks, both Dinah and Jacob would have been around six or seven years old when leaving Paddan Aram.

The period of time from Jacob's arrival in Canaan until the rape of his daughter is uncertain but it happened before the birth of Benjamin which was subsequently preceded Joseph being sold into slavery at age 17. If one assumes that Shechem was only a rapist and not also a child molester, then Dinah would have to have been around the age to be considered for marriage. This is further bolstered by the fact that after the rape Shechem wanted her as his wife. The same supposition for Dinah will be made as with Rebecca when she married Isaac and Rachel on her first encounter with Jacob around 15 or 16 years old.

As Jacob's family hastily left Shechem for Beckel, Deborah, Rebecca's nurse, who for some unknown reason was traveling with them died and was buried just outside Beckel (Genesis 35:1-8). They moved on from Beckel toward Ephrath (Bethlehem) and Rachel went into labor and died in childbirth giving birth to Benjamin. Jacob buried her by the road to Ephrath and he put a special rock on her grave to honor her (Genesis 35:16-19).

Based on the preceding analysis it will be assumed that Joseph was at least 15 and possibly 16 years older than Benjamin.

Shortly after the death of Rachel, Jacob suffered another heart wrenching event. Reuben, his first born is said to have slept with Bilhah, Rachel's servant who was also one of Jacob's concubines. Jacob heard of it and was very angry (Genesis 35:21). It eventually led to Reuben's right of inheritance as the first born being stripped from him and given to Joseph (Genesis 48:22, 49:2-4) while the position of clan leadership was conveyed to Judah (Genesis 49:9-10).

Every sex story, even old ones, fuels the tabloids. An internet search of the names Reuben and Bilhah brings up beaucoup hits. At least one says Reuben and Bilhah were using each other to their own advantage: Reuben to assert his birth right and Bilhah to go directly to the eventual head of household and assert herself as chief wife. However a more interesting one is put forth by a group of Rabbis who claim that no actual sexual encounter took place. They claim that while Rachel was alive, Jacob's bed was always in Rachel's tent which asserted her position as chief wife. They say that on her death, Jacob moved his bed to Bilhah's tent. They claim that Reuben resented this and substituted his mother Leah's bed for Bilhah's and this is what Jacob refers to as Reuben defiling his bed (Genesis 49:4).

The foregoing episode makes the assertion that Bilhah and the assumption that Leah and possible Zilpah were still alive at the death of Rachel. The date and time of Leah's death is not given but presumably it occurred after Jacob had settled in an area near where his father Isaac and grandfather Abraham had stayed because when he was about to die in Egypt he asked to be taken back to be buried with his ancestors in the family grave. This is the cave of Machpelah that Abraham bought from Ephron the Hittite to bury Sarah. Jacob stated that Abraham and Sarah, Isaac and Rebekah were buried there and that is where he buried Leah (Genesis 49:31). There appears to be no record as to when or where either Bilhah or Zilpah died or where either was buried.

COMMENTARY NO. 14

Joseph-From Slave to Governor

At the age of seventeen, Joseph was the apple of his father's eye. To say that he was the child of his old age misses the point. By using Joseph's age when he rose to power and Jacob's age when he came into Egypt, it is possible to calculate that he was about 90 years old when Joseph was born. But since all 12 of Jacob's children born in Paddan Aram were born within a seven year period, he would have been around 83 years old when Reuben the eldest was born. A child of his old age would be more aptly applied to Benjamin, his only child born in Canaan who would have been a toddler of about two at the time. It is probable that the real reason Joseph got Jacob's attention as did anyone with authority over him was his apparent ability to analyze the inputs of any situation and from it devise the proper course of action. That is another way of saying he was a natural born leader. Jacob gave Joseph an ornate long sleeved multicolored robe. It is referred to in many bible versions as a "coat of many colors." Joseph's brothers resented him. Perhaps out of jealousy for their father's affinity for Joseph or the way Jacob relied on him for information about what was going on with his flocks. One day Joseph gave Jacob a bad report on the sons of Bilhah and Zilpah which enhanced their resentment of him (Genesis 37:2-4).

One day Joseph had a dream which he told to his brothers. He said that in his dream they were all binding sheaths of wheat. When they finished, his sheath stood up and all of their sheaths bowed down before his sheath. His brothers said do you think you will be ruler over us and they resented him even more. Then Joseph had another dream. In this dream, he said the sun, moon and twelve stars were bowing to him. He told this dream to his brothers and also to Jacob. Jacob rebuked him saying do you think your mother and I and all your brothers will be ruled by you. Jacob's reply is a little puzzling since his mother was already dead. His daughter's Dinah's name seems as if it would have been more appropriate (Genesis 37:5-11).

One day, the brothers sans Joseph were grazing Jacob's flocks near Shechem. Jacob decides to send Joseph to see how his brothers and his flocks were doing. When Joseph came near Shechem, a stranger told him that his brothers had moved on to Dothan and he went on to find them there. The brothers saw him coming from afar and plotted to kill him and to pretend that some wild animal had done it. Reuben, possibly out of a sense of entitlement of being the first born to be in charge or to help square himself of his little tryst with Bilhah said he is our brother, lets not kill him, lets throw him in one of these dry wells. Reuben had intentions of later pulling Joseph out of the well and sending him home to Jacob (Genesis 37:12-24).

After putting Joseph in the well, the somewhat heartless brothers sat down to eat. Reuben had apparently wandered off somewhere because he was not present. Just as they started to eat they looked up and saw a caravan of Ishmaelites coming by from Gilead on their way to Egypt. Judah, either out of a surge of compassion or saw way to make a few quick shekels said we should not kill him. After all he is our own brother. He said lets sell him to those Midianite[1] traders (Genesis 37:25-27). So Joseph at the age of seventeen was sold to the traders for 20 shekels of silver and carried down to Egypt. When Reuben returned and found Joseph missing from the well he tore his clothes in anguish. The brothers killed a goat and dipped Joseph's coat in its blood. They took the coat to Jacob and said we found this coat, is it Joseph's. Jacob said "yes, some wild animal must have torn him to pieces." He then tore his clothes and put on sackcloth and mourned for many days. (Genesis 37:28-35).

In Egypt, the Midanite traders sold Joseph to Potiphar the commander of Pharaoh's palace guard (Genesis 37:36). Some versions of the bible also named him as the chief executioner. One referred to him as the butcher. It didn't take long for Potiphar to recognize the leadership qualities of Jacob and placed him in charge of all the servants in his household (Genesis 39:1-6).

In spite of being a slave, Joseph held a fairly enviable position. This lasted until Potiphar's wife cast her eyes upon him and noticed how handsome he was. She tried to get Joseph to come to bed with her. Day after day she tried but Joseph always refused telling her he could not do such an evil thing. One day Joseph went in the house to perform his duties and found himself alone in the house with Potiphar's wife. She physically grabbed him and tried to pull him to her bed. Joseph broke loose leaving his robe behind. Potiphar's wife was apparently so angered by the rejection she called the other servants in and said "This Hebrew slave tried to rape me." She told the same story to her husband when he arrived at home. Potiphar had Joseph put in the palace prison (Genesis 39:7-20). It is said that the prison warden recognized Joseph's leadership and placed him in charge of all the other prisoners (Genesis 39:21-23).

It is possible to speculate that Potiphar might have had doubts about who cast eyes on whom. He was the head executioner and did not execute the person that his wife had accused of attempting to rape her. Although he may not have had full authority as to whom was to be executed, in a situation such as this he is bound to have had a great deal of influence. It is also possible that Potiphar not the warden placed Joseph in charge of all the prisoners. It may have been that he did not want to lose the services of a good leader but he just had to keep Joseph out of the sight his wife. This is further bolstered by the fact that when Pharaoh's two officials were put in prison, it was Potiphar not the warden that placed them under Joseph's care (Genesis 40:4).

The two officials referred in the preceding paragraph were the Pharaoh's chief cup bearer[2] and chief baker. They had somehow angered the pharaoh and he had them put in prison. After they had been there for quite some time, they both had dreams on the same night. The next morning when Joseph came to them he asked why they were so dejected. They said we both had dreams and didn't know what they meant. Joseph said "only God knows the meaning of dreams but tell me your dreams." The cup bearer said, "I dreamed that I was facing a grapevine with three branches. Each branch flowered then bore fruit and ripened right away. I took the fruit and squeezed the grapes into Pharaoh's cup." Joseph said, "Your dream means that in the three days Pharaoh will lift you up and pardon you and you will again pour the wine into Pharaoh's cup. When you do, remember me to the Pharaoh because I was forcibly carried away from the land of the Hebrews and I do not belong here." (Genesis 40:5-15).

After hearing a favorable dream interpretation for the cupbearer, the baker decided to give it a try. The baker said, "I dreamed I was walking with three baskets on my head one on top of the other. The top basket was filled with all types of good thing to eat. But the birds came and picked at the food in the basket. Joseph said, "Your dream means that in the three days Pharaoh will lift you up and cut off your head. The birds will come along and pick at your flesh." (Genesis 40:16-19).

Three days later was the Pharaoh's birthday. He gave a big celebration invited all his officials. Then Pharaoh's action toward the cupbearer and baker were as Joseph had predicted, but the cupbearer never mentioned Joseph to the Pharaoh (Genesis 40:20-23).

Two years later the Pharaoh was having very troubling dreams. He assembled all his magicians and wise men but no one could tell him what the dreams meant. Then the cupbearer remembered Joseph. He said to Pharaoh, "When the baker and I were in prison, there was a young Hebrew prisoner that accurately interpreted the dreams of each of us." The Pharaoh said "Bring him to me." (Genesis 41:1-13).

Joseph was allowed to shave and given new clothes in which to dress and brought before the Pharaoh. The Pharaoh said to Joseph, "I have been having dreams and no one can tell me their meaning. I have been told that you can tell the meaning of dreams." Joseph answered, "Only God can tell the meaning of dreams but tell them to me." The Pharaoh then said, "I dreamed that seven fat cows came up of the river and were grazing on the lush green grass on the shore. Then seven more cows poor and lean came up out of the river and devoured the seven fat cows and they were still poor and lean. Then I awakened. I fell asleep again and I dreamed there were seven heads of grain[3] on a single stalk full and ripe standing in the field. Then seven more heads of grain dry and parched by the east wind came on to the stalk and devoured the seven full ripe heads of grain." (Genesis 41:14-24). Joseph said, "The two dreams mean the same thing. God is telling you that there will seven years of plenty in the land followed by seven years of famine and it is repeated because God is certain about it and it is going to happen soon." (Genesis 41:25-32).

The Pharaoh said what can I do? Joseph answered, "You should appoint a wise and discerning man and place him in charge of all Egypt. Then you should appoint overseers to gather one-fifth of all grain grown around each city during the seven years of plenty and place it in fortified storehouses in the cities under the authority of the Pharaoh. Then during the seven years of famine there will be grain available to keep the people alive" (Genesis 41:33-36).

The Pharaoh said to Joseph "since God has made known all these things to you; I don't think we can find a wiser or more discerning man than you." All of his officials agreed. The Pharaoh then said "Therefore I appoint you Joseph to be in charge of all Egypt. Only in matters of the throne will I be above you." He dressed Joseph in fine linen, gave him a ring from his finger with the seal of authority and placed a gold chain around his neck. He also gave him as a wife Asenath the daughter of Potiphera priest of On (Genesis 41:37-45). This is yet another example of the immediate recognition and application of Joseph's leadership abilities. Joseph was thirty years old when he entered into the service of the Pharaoh. He traveled throughout the entire country of Egypt getting things established. So much food was placed in the store houses during the years of plenty it became impossible to measure. Prior to the years of famine, Asenath bore Joseph two sons. He named the eldest Manasseh and the younger one Ephraim (Genesis 41:46-52).

After the years of plenty, the years of famine began. The famine was not just in Egypt but the surrounding countries as well. As the Famine progressed and the people of Egypt found themselves without food, they cried out to Pharaoh for help. He told them to go to Joseph and do what he says (Genesis 41:53-55).

Footnotes:

1. The Terms Ishmaelites and Midianites are used interchangeably in different versions of the bible with Ishmaelites most often used as the name of the caravan and Midianites most often used to describe the traders but the reverse is also used. Both the Ishmaelites and Midianites were descendants of Abraham. The Expanded bible version says that Midian was a part of the Ishmaelite nation.

2. In addition to cup bearer this official is referred to in some versions as butler, personal servant, wine steward or wine server. The baker in at least one version is called cook. In a couple of versions, both officials were referred to as eunuchs.

3. Instead of "heads of grain," many versions of the bible especially the older ones use "ears of corn" and a fair number use the hybrid versions "ears of grain." On the internet there is an article titled "Origin, History and Uses of Corn" by Lance Gibson and Garren Bensen of Iowa State University, Department of Agronomy. The following paragraph from that article is reproduced here in its entirety: "The word "corn" has many different meanings depending what country you are in. Corn in the United States is also called maize or Indian corn. In some countries, corn means the leading crop grown in a certain district. Corn in England means wheat; in Scotland and Ireland, it refers to oats. Corn mentioned in the Bible probably refers to wheat or barley."

Commentary No. 15

Jacob's Sons go to Egypt to buy Grain

As Joseph had predicted (Commentary 14) Egypt had seven years of bountiful harvests. Joseph went about doing what had to be done to store grain for the lean years to come. After about two years of famine the Egyptians began to run out of grain. They went to Joseph who sold them grain from the store houses. When their money ran out they traded their livestock for grain when they had no more livestock, they sold themselves to Pharaoh as indentured servants (Genesis 47:13-26).

Meanwhile, the famine was being felt throughout the surrounding countries. It was being felt in Canaan some 300 miles away where Jacob and his family had settled. About two years into the famine, Jacob had learned by what ever means that served as broadband communications at the time that there was grain for sale in Egypt. He told his sons to take some money and pack mules and go down to Egypt and buy some grain so that their family could be kept alive. So all the brothers present except the youngest Benjamin set off for Egypt (Genesis 42:1-5).

When the brothers arrived in Egypt and went to buy grain, Joseph recognized them but they did not recognize him. Apparently just to mess with their heads a little, he accused them through an interpreter of being spies come to check on Egypt's vulnerabilities in advance of an invading army. They replied, oh no, we are all brothers the sons of one man. The youngest is home with our father and one is no more. He had them all confined to jail. Reuben complained to the others, "This is all happening because of what we did to Joseph. I told you we should not have harmed the boy."

Two days later, Joseph had the brothers brought before him. He indicated that he was leaning toward believing their story, sort of. He told them all they had to do to prove their case was to go and bring back their youngest brother. And by the way, I will keep one of you here until that happens. He chose Simeon, tied him up and sent him back to prison. He had all the brothers' sacks filled with grain (presumably that included Simeon's sacks) and sent them on their way. At one point on the way home when they stopped to rest, one of the brothers reached in one of his sacks to get grain to feed his pack mule he found that the silver he had taken to buy grain had been returned in his sack. Eventually after arriving home, they each found their silver had been returned in their sacks (Genesis 42:6-28).

Upon arrival of the brothers back home, the story of their encounter with the Governor of Egypt was relayed to Jacob. They told him that the only way to clear their suspicion of being spies and to secure the release of Simeon was to return to the Governor with Benjamin. Jacob indicated that since Benjamin was the only remaining son of his beloved wife Rachel that he could not let him go. Reuben then offered to let him take Benjamin and if he didn't bring the boy home safely that Jacob could kill his two sons (Genesis 42:29-37).

This is yet another assertion (as in Commentary no.10 when Jacob said that anyone found with Laban's Gods would be put to death) that the head of household held absolute sway of life or death of its members. Reuben also seems not to be taking into account the punishment he would receive in the killing of his two sons also punishes Jacob who would be losing two grandsons.

As the grain the brothers had brought began to run out, hunger and the threat of starvation again beset Jacob's clan. Jacob asked the brothers to go back to Egypt and buy more grain. They refused. Judah said the man said we would not see his face if we did not bring our youngest brother with us. Judah said he would assume personal responsibility for the boy's welfare if Jacob would let him go. Reluctantly Jacob allowed Benjamin to go. He said "Return the money you found in your sacks. Perhaps it was a mistake. Take new money to buy grain. Take the man a gift of some of the good things we have here such as spices, balm, almonds and honey." (Genesis 43:1-15).

So the brothers, including Benjamin, left for Egypt. When they arrived they told the Steward that they had come once again to buy grain. They also told him that they had returned the money they someone had apparently mistakenly placed in their sacks. The steward said your god must have put the money in your sacks for I received full payment for the grain. When Joseph learned his brothers had arrived. He planned to have lunch with them.

The brothers spent the morning preparing the gifts they had brought (Genesis 42:16-23).

At lunch, Simeon was brought to join the other brothers. The brothers brought in their presents and bowed before Joseph. Joseph said your father you spoke of is he well? He looked toward Benjamin and said. "Is this your youngest brother? May God be gracious to you my son." Joseph was so overcome with emotion on seeing Benjamin he had to leave the room and weep. After he composed himself he returned to the room. The Egyptians all sat at one table because they consider it an abomination to eat with Hebrews. Joseph sat at a table by himself and the brothers all sat at a table facing him. They were amazed when they realized that they had been seated in birth order from the eldest to the youngest. The servants took food from Joseph's table to the brothers' table but Benjamin received five times as much food as the other brothers (Genesis 43:24-34).

When the brothers were ready to return home, Joseph instructed his steward to place each ones silver in his sack of grain and to also place Joseph's silver cup in Benjamin's sack. After they had traveled as much as they could for the day and stopped to rest, they were accosted by Joseph's servants and asked why did you steal our master cup? It is the cup he uses for divination. They said we did not steal your master's cup. Search our baggage and if anyone has the cup, that person may be put to death and the rest of us will be his slaves. The servant said only the one who has the cup will be made a slave the rest of you will be allowed to go free. The servants searched the brothers' sacks starting with the eldest one by one and of course they found the cup in Benjamin's sack. The brothers all tore their clothes in anguish (Genesis 44:1-13).

The brothers with all their goods and pack animals were returned to Joseph. Joseph said, "Didn't you know that a man like me could tell what you were doing by divination. Then Judah began his elegant plea for Benjamin's release (Genesis 44:18-34). He pleaded that the boy be allowed to return to his father. He offered himself as a slave in lieu of Benjamin. The reason he gave is that their father's life was so wrapped up with the boy the only remaining son of his mother, her other son had been killed by a wild animal, that to lose him would surely send him to his grave.

Finally Joseph could no longer restrain himself. He sent all of the Egyptian servants out of the room and began to sob loudly. He started speaking to his brothers in their own language. "He said I am Joseph whom you sold years ago. He said how is my father? Is he still alive?" He embraced Benjamin and cried a long time. Then he told the other brothers to come closer to him and he kissed each of them. At first the brothers were bewildered and speechless but finally they believed Joseph and started talking. He told them don't be angry with yourselves for what you did God intended it for good so that I would be able to save many lives. There are still five more years of this famine. Go and bring my father and your families here I will provide a place for you in the land of Goshen the fertile Nile delta region. Tell my father that I am in charge of all of Egypt. I am like a father to Pharaoh. The Egyptians that were sent from the room overheard and told Pharaoh. He and his officials were very pleased that Joseph's brothers had come. The Pharaoh also agreed with Joseph on bringing his family to Egypt (Genesis 45:1-20).

Joseph provided good wagons and provisions for his father and his brother's families. He gave each of his brothers a fine suit of clothes but he gave Benjamin five suits of clothes. He told his brothers to hurry home and not to quarrel with each other on the way. It seems as if he had prior experience in that area (Genesis 45:21-28).

COMMENTARY No. 16

Jacob's Family Moves to Egypt

When the Brothers arrived home after their second trip to Egypt to buy grain and told Jacob that Joseph was alive and in charge of all of Egypt he did not believe them. But when he saw all the good wagons and provision he had sent, he started believe. He said "to be able to see Joseph once again, I can die in peace." Jacob and his sons made preparations and loaded their families and belongings on the wagons and set out for Egypt herding all their livestock along.

The direct descendants of Jacob that came into Egypt not counting their wives were sixty six. These are enumerated in Genesis 46:8-25 ordered by birth mother and sequential by child birth order for the given mother. First is Leah and her children followed in order by Zilpah, then Rachel and finally Bilhah. Not all of the descendants will be repeated here, only those for which commentaries will be rendered.

The first will be Reuben. Genesis 46: 9 reads "And the sons of Reubin: Hanoch, Pallu, Hezron, and Carmi." When Reuben made the offer to Jacob that if he did not return from Egypt with Benjamin, he could kill his two sons (Genesis 42:37). Which two sons? It shows here he had four sons unless two were born in the very short period of time after the assertion was made.

The second will be Simeon. Genesis 46:10 reads "The sons of Simeon: Jemuel, Jamin, Ohad, Jachin, Zohar and Shaul the son of a Canaanite woman." Wait a minute! Jacob spent seven years with Laban without being married. Then he somehow conceived twelve children with four women in the next seven years. He then spent six more years building up his own herds. Therefore, all of his children would have been under thirteen years old when arriving in Canaan. Wouldn't all of his sons' wives be Canaanite women? The following discussion of Judah specifically states that he and married the daughter of a Canaanite man named Shuah.

The third will be Judah. Genesis 46:12 reads: "The sons of Judah: Er, Onan, Shelah, Perez and Zerah ; but Er and Onan died in the land of Canaan. And the sons of Perez, were Hezron and Hamul." An entire chapter (Genesis 38) is devoted to the development of Judah's family while separated from his brothers. The story is that he had befriended and was spending time with an Adullamite man named Hirah. While there he met and married the daughter of a Canaanite man named Shuah. His wife bore him three sons in order Er, Onan and Shelah. He chose a wife for his first born Er. Her name was Tamar. Er was wicked in the eyes of the Lord so he took his life. Then Judah told Onan marry his brother's widow and raise up children in his name. But Onan knew the children would not be his so when he slept with her he avoided conception. The Lord considered this wicked and slew him also. Judah told Tamar to don her widow's clothes and return to her father's house until Shelah grew up and he would be given to her as her husband. As Shelah grew up, Judah, fearing the same fate might befall him as his other sons, did not give him to Tamar.

Sometime later Judah's wife died. After a time of mourning, Judah was going with his friend Hirah to Timnath to shear his sheep. Tamar, realizing that Shelah had grown up and had not been given to her to wed, found out that Judah was going to shear sheep and the path he was going to take. She dressed as a prostitute with her face covered as was their custom and sat by the side of the road by which Judah would pass. When Judah saw her there he negotiated a deal with her for her services. She asked him what he was willing to pay for her services. He offered her a young goat but since he did not have it with him, she asked for a good faith pledge. Specifically, she asked for his staff and his signet ring and its cord. Judah's friend Hirah took the goat by the place where Tamar was suppose to be but could not find her.

Three months later, Judah hears that Tamar is pregnant by harlotry. He says to bring her forth and burn her to death. When she was brought forth, she produced the pledge Judah had given her and said "I am pregnant by the man to whom these belong." Judah then realized that he was more at fault than she by withholding Shelah and called off the burning. Six months later Tamar gave gives birth to twins Perez and Zerah but Judah did not cohabit with her again.

This synopsis of Genesis 38 was presented to show that father-son relationship between Judah and Perez and Zerah is equivalent in age difference to a grandfather-grandson relationship since either ER, Onan or even Shelah were old enough to have been the father of Perez and Zerah. Therefore Perez's sons Hezron and Hamul, Judah's grandsons were equivalent in age to being his great-grandsons. It seems some what incredulous that four generations could have taken place in the given time span. Since at this point Joseph was estimated to be around forty years old give or take a few months and even his eldest brother Reuben could be no more than seven years older than Joseph and Judah being the fourth born would probably be in his early forties.

There are two possible ways out of the time crunch dilemma. One, the time spent with Laban was not reported correctly and the difference in age between Joseph and Judah was greater than indicated. Or Joseph was older than the forty or so years being estimated. This would be true if there is a time gap between when Joseph started serving the Pharaoh at the age of thirty and when the seven years of plenty began. This is essentially between Genesis 41:46 and Genesis 41:47. It is stated in verse 46 that Joseph went out from Pharaoh and traveled throughout the land of Egypt. How long did this take? What was he doing? Did he have to oversee the construction of storehouses that would keep grain palatable from the time of plenty to the end of the seven lean years? In Commentary 12 there was the obvious unreported time gap in Jacob moving from Sukkoth to Shechem. Could this also be an unstated time gap? It seems plausible.

The fourth to be considered will be Asher. Genesis 46:17 reads: "The sons of Asher: Imnah, Ishvah, Ishvi, Beriah, and Serah their sister. And the sons of Beriah: Heber and Malchiel." Asher is the only brother besides Judah to have grandchildren and the only one to have a daughter. Dinah, Jacob's daughter born to Leah and Asher's daughter Serah are only females among Jacob's sixty six direct descendants that came into Egypt and the three direct descendants that were already there. This being a time and culture that favored male descendants, leads one to wonder if there was possibly some overt suppression of female offspring.

The fifth and final to be considered is Benjamin. Genesis 46:21 reads: "And the sons of Benjamin: Bela, Becher, Ashbel, Gera, Naaman, Ehi, Rosh, Muppim, Huppim, and Ard." The way Benjamin was referred to as the boy or the lad by his brothers; one would think they were describing a prepubescent teenager. But as can be seen he came into Egypt the father of ten sons, the most sons of any of the brothers. It was determined in Commentary no.12 that he was probably about fifteen years younger than Joseph, therefore Benjamin was around twenty five or possibly older if Joseph was older than forty as the preceding speculation would have it. It is also possible that Jacob was so concerned about possible harm befalling Benjamin that he kept him near the home base and did not allow him to go out herding with his brothers. Consequently he had more time to hang around the tents and procreate. There is no indication of how many wives and/or how many concubines he had if any.

After the family entered Egypt, Joseph coached his brothers to say that they were shepherds so that the Pharaoh would allow them to use the fertile grazing land of Goshen. He chose five of his brothers to meet the Pharaoh. Then Joseph brought his father in. Jacob blessed the Pharaoh. Then The Pharaoh asked Jacob how old he was. He answered that he was 130 years old and sort of complained how hard his life had been and sort of hinting that he was not likely to live as long as his fore bearers. His Grandfather Abraham had lived to be 175 and his father Isaac lived to be 180.

After Jacob had lived in Egypt for seventeen years and was nearing the end of his life he called for Joseph. He got Joseph to swear that he would not bury him in Egypt. He wanted to be buried in Canaan in the family grave where his ancestors were buried. Sometime later, Joseph heard that Jacob was sick and he went to see him. Joseph took his son Manasseh and Ephraim with him. Jacob said to Joseph. I claim these two sons as my own. Any other children born to you will be yours. Joseph then brought in his sons for Jacob to bless them. He placed Manasseh at Jacob's right and Ephraim on his left. But Jacob crossed his hands and placed his right hand on Ephraim's head and his left hand on Manasseh. When Joseph protested that Manasseh was the first born, Jacob said. "I know but his brother will be greater than he." Then Jacob elevated Joseph's status among his brothers. He said "I will give you a sliver of land which is not shared with any of your brothers." This land is alternatively referred to as mountain ridge, mountain slope and Shechem in various versions of the bible.

Then Jacob uttered a statement that appears somewhat controversial. He said "This is land I took from the Amorites with my sword and my bow." Looking back through the bible from Jacob's birth until the time of his impending death, there is no indication of his ever using his sword of bow against anyone. There was that incident where Simeon and Levi went in and slew all the men of Shechem while they were sore from circumcision and they with their brothers made off with all their possessions including their women and children (Commentary No. 12). It is possible and quite probable that Jacob was referring to this encounter. But the truth of the matter is he spoke disapprovingly and with great trepidation at the time of what his sons had done fearing a possible attack from the surrounding tribes (Genesis 34:30).

When Jacob was about to die he summoned all of his sons to his bed side. He uttered in birth order a prognostication to each son of his progeny. He took Reuben's birthright as head of the family and gave it to Judah (Genesis 49:8-10). It should be mentioned that Jacob in addition to giving Joseph the extra sliver land, by making Joseph's sons his own, Jacob also gave Joseph's progeny a double share of the land that Israel was to inherit[1]. When Jacob had finished his prognostications, he pulled his feet up into the bed and joined his ancestors. Joseph threw himself on his father and cried for a long time (Genesis 50:1).

In accordance with his fathers wishes, he had Jacob embalmed. The process took forty days in the manner of the Egyptians. Then Jacob's entire family except for small children and livestock joined in the trip to take Jacob to the family burial place. When they reached a threshing floor they stopped and lamented for seven days then they proceeded to the burial place (Genesis 50:2-11).

After Jacob was buried and the families all returned to Egypt, Joseph's brothers feared that now that their father was dead that Joseph might seek revenge on them for what they had done to him. They concocted a story and went to Joseph and said that our father said you should forgive us for the wrong we did to you and they bowed before him and offered themselves as his slaves. On hearing this Joseph began to cry. By now, it must be obvious that Joseph was a crier. Joseph said what you did you meant for evil but God meant it for good that I might be able to save many lives. He assured them that he would always provide for them and their families (Genesis 50:15-21). Joseph continued living in Egypt until his death at age 110. He said when god takes us out of this land to the land promised to our forefathers; take my body with you (Genesis 50:22-26).

Footnote:

1. The twelve tribes of Israel included tribes of Manasseh and Ephraim. There was no Josephite tribe or Levite tribe. The Levites were designated to take care of the priestly duties of all the other tribes. This happened after Moses was told by God to perform an act of literal nepotism and appoint his brother Aaron and Aaron's sons as priests (Exodus 28).

Genesis Genealogy

Adam
(Eve)

Cain   Abel   Seth
               Enosh
               Kenan
               Mahalael
               Jared
               Enoch
               Methusaleh
               Lamech
               Noah

Japheth   **Shem**   Ham

Japhethites   Arphaxad   Hamites (includes Canaan)
               Shelah
               Eber
               Peleg
               Reu
               Serug
               Nahor
               Terah

Haran   Nahor   **Abraham**
               →(Milkah)
               Bethuel

Lot
(Iskah)?   Laban←

(Daughter1) (Daughter2)   →(Sarah)   (Hagar)   (Keturah)
Moab   Ben-Ammi   **Isaac**   Ishmael   8 sons
Moabites   Ammonites   →(Rebekah)   Ishmaelites

               Jacob   Esau
                                              (3 wives)
                                              Edomites

(Leah)←   →(Rachel)   (Zilpah)   (Bilhah)

Reubin Simeon Levi Judah Issachar Zebulun (Dinah) **Joseph** Benjamin Gad Asher Dan Naphtali

51

Printed in the United States
By Bookmasters

ISBN 978-1-5049-2497-
5129

authorHOUSE®

Dr. Shokhan Rasool Ahmed

MAGIC *and* GENERDER
in
EARLY MODERN
ENGLAND
RENAISSANCE DRAMA